LET'S LOOK AT...

Flowers and Plants

OF THE BRITISH ISLES

Lucy Beevor

raintree

a Capstone company — publishers for children

Raintree is an imprint of Capstone Global Library Limited, a company incorporated in England and Wales having its registered office at 264 Banbury Road, Oxford, OX2 7DY – Registered company number: 6695582

www.raintree.co.uk
myorders@raintree.co.uk

Edited by Clare Lewis
Designed by Cynthia Della-Rovere
Original illustrations © Capstone Global Library Limited 2018
Picture research by Jo Miller
Production by Tori Abraham
Originated by Capstone Global Library Ltd
Printed and bound in India

ISBN 978 1 4747 6386 8
22 21 20 19 18
10 9 8 7 6 5 4 3 2 1

British Library Cataloguing in Publication Data
A full catalogue record for this book is available from the British Library.

Acknowledgements
We would like to thank the following for permission to reproduce photographs: Dreamstime: Stig Karlsson, 17 BL; Shutterstock: 3rn4, 5 BL, Agata Kowalczyk, 18 Top, Alan Bryant, 5 TL, alybaba, 24 Bottom, Andrew Buckin, 13 BL, Andrey Skaternoy, 3 TL, 14 BR, ANGHI, 14 TL, Anna Gratys, 19 Left, 32, Arie v.d. Wolde, 8 BR, Ariena, 26 Top, arousa, 20 TR, Arto Hakola, 19 Right, BerndBrueggemann, 21 Top, Burkhard Trautsch, 29 Left, Chris Moody, 5 TM, ChWeiss, 18 BL, Claudio Divizia, 12 Bottom, Cora Mueller, 17 Middle, Cyrustr, 14 TR, Dancestrokes, 15 Bottom, Dmitry Sheremeta, 3 TR, 10 Bottom, Donna Carpenter, 22 Bottom, Eileen Kumpf, Cover Back, 7 BL, Elliotte Rusty Harold, 17 Top, Fire-fly, 7 TL, fl_level, 23 BR, footageclips, 8 Top, garmoncheg, 24 Top, Gherzak, 22 Top, GraphicsRF, 11 Bottom, Gurcharan Singh, 28 BR, Helen Hotson, 4 Bottom, Henrik Larsson, 18 BR, IanRedding, 25 Top, Ida-Mari Henriksen, 14 BL, James W Copeland, 7 ML, Jolanda Aalbers, 3 BL, 23 BL, Kicky_princess, 15 Top, kukuruxa, Cover Bottom, 1, lansa, 3 BR, 27 BR, Laura Bartlett, 28 BL, Leighton Collins, 20 Bottom, lek2481, Cover TL, Leonid Andronov, 5 MB, Lipatova Maryna, 10 Top, Liz Miller, 7 BR, Mark Heighes, 6 Top, Martin Fowler, 6 BR, 7 TR, 8 BL, 12 Top, 20 TL, MaryAnne Campbell, 25 MR, Morten Normann Almeland, 7 MR, mubus7, 5 BR, natalia bulatova, 27 BL, Nick Reynolds Photography, 4 Top, Ninell Creative, 10 Middle, nnnnae, Design Element, Ole Schoener, 25 Bottom, On the Move, 26 BR, PARINYA ART, 16 Bottom, Peter Turner Photography, 9 Bottom, PJ photography, 16 Middle, PRILL, 13 TL, Przemyslaw Muszynski, 13 TR, Ricky Howitt, Cover TM, Rob Bayer, 28 TL, Sample Stars, 27 Top, Sarah Weldon FRGS, 23 TR, Sarah2, 25 ML, Shulevskyy Volodymyr, 11 Top, sparc, 9 Middle, Split Second Stock, 17 BR, Stefan Holm, 21 Bottom, Stefano Garau, 16 Top, Stephen Farhall, 9 TL, Suparak FOTO, 26 BL, Tatiana Volgutova, 29 TR, Tessa Bishop, 5 TR, Tom Curtis, Cover TR, Triff, 29 BR, Vahan Abrahamyan, 13 BR, Visharo, 6 BL, 31, vvvita, 28 TR, ZuzaHre, 23 TL.

Contents

Let's look at British flowers and plants 4

Woodlands 6

Hedgerows 10

Grasslands 12

Freshwater habitats 16

Along the coast 18

Heathland and mountains 22

Towns and cities 24

Parks and gardens 26

Glossary 30

Find out more 31

Index 32

Some words are shown in bold, **like this**. You can find out what they mean by looking in the glossary.

LET'S LOOK AT
British flowers and plants

woodlands

along the coast

Flowers and plants are an important part of our world. There are thousands of types of wildflowers and plants in Britain. We also grow and care for plants and flowers in gardens and parks.

Different plants grow and **thrive** in different places. From stony beaches to shady hedgerows, this book will show you where to spot some common flowers and other plants!

Plant habitats

A habitat is a place where an animal or plant lives. Britain has lots of different habitats. Plants grow in the habitat that suits them best. Here are some of the main habitats for flowers and plants in the British Isles.

We have grouped the plants under the habitats where they are often found. But you may see them elsewhere too. Keep your eyes open. You never know where you might spot a wildflower!

hedgerows

grasslands

freshwater habitats

mountains and heathlands

towns and cities

gardens and parks

What do plants need to grow?

WATER Flowers and plants suck up water through their roots. They also take in water through their leaves.

NUTRIENTS The roots take in **nutrients**, like food, from soil and water.

LIGHT Light from the sun carries energy. Flowers use this energy to make their food. This is called **photosynthesis**.

CARBON DIOXIDE This is a gas in the air. Plants take in carbon dioxide through tiny holes in their leaves.

THE RIGHT TEMPERATURE Plants can only grow in the right temperature for them. If it gets too hot they could shrivel up and die. When it gets too cold in winter, most plants die back. They often grow again in the spring.

Woodlands

Woodlands are large areas of land covered with tall trees. A huge variety of flowers and plants grow in the shady, damp ground beneath the trees.

WILD GARLIC

Wild garlic has a strong smell. You might smell it before you see it! Clumps of wild garlic grow in woodlands, covering the ground in white flowers.

BLUEBELL

In the springtime, thousands of bluebells bloom in the UK's woodlands. Their purple-blue, bell-shaped flowers cover the forest floor like a colourful carpet!

PRIMROSE

Primroses grow in small clusters on the forest floor. The flowers have five yellow petals. Their leaves are hairy underneath.

FORGET-ME-NOT

Forget-me-nots have small, **delicate** blue flowers. The flowers grow low to the ground. They can spread around other plants over a large area.

WOOD ANENOME

Hoverflies and other insects are attracted to the wood anenome's white flowers.

SNAKE'S HEAD FRITILLARY

This flower is unusual. Its petals are covered in purple and white squares that look a bit like snake's skin!

LORDS AND LADIES

This plant has bright red berries in the autumn. Its leaves are green with cream marbling. It grows well in damp shade beneath trees.

LILY OF THE VALLEY

This pretty plant usually grows in dry woodlands. The white bell-like flowers have a strong sweet smell.

EARLY PURPLE ORCHID

The flowers on this plant grow in a cone-shaped cluster on a tall spike. There can be up to 50 flowers on one spike.

DEADLY NIGHTSHADE

The flowers of deadly nightshade are shaped like green and purple bells. They look pretty but this plant really is deadly! The black berries that appear on this plant in autumn are very **poisonous**.

MISTLETOE

Mistletoe is a plant that grows on other trees. Its roots cling to the tree's bark. Soon they break through the bark. The mistletoe then gets food and water from inside the tree. You may see balls of mistletoe growing on trees in the south and west Midlands of the UK. People decorate their homes with mistletoe at Christmas.

FLY AGARIC

You may know this plant by its other name – the toadstool! It is a large, red mushroom with white spots. Toadstools sometimes grow in circles. The circles are called fairy rings.

YELLOW BRAIN FUNGUS

This jelly-like **fungus** grows on rotten wood. Its bright yellow colour makes it easy to spot.

CARPET MOSS

This golden-green moss covers the ground, just like a carpet. The moss is soft and warm. Squirrels use carpet moss to make their dreys (nests) warm and cosy.

BRAMBLES

Brambles are thorny **shrubs**. Pinky-white flowers cover the shrub in the summer. In the late summer, blackberries are ready to pick.

Hedgerows

Hedgerows are long rows of bushes. They often separate fields from roads or paths. Hedges are usually a mix of **shrubs** and trees, such as hawthorn, blackthorn and hazel. Wildflowers and plants grow among the trees and shrubs.

GOOSEGRASS

This very sticky plant grows very quickly. It has tiny hooked bristles on its stem, leaves and seeds. The bristles cling to clothing or to animal fur.

SNOWDROP

Snowdrops are white, bell-shaped flowers. They are one of the first flowers to grow in spring. Their green shoots push through the last of the winter snow.

IVY

Ivy is a climbing plant. Hairs on the stems help it to stick to walls, trees and plants as it grows up them. It does not die back in the winter, so you can see its glossy leaves all year round.

RED CAMPION

Red campion adds colour to hedgerows in the spring and summer. Its bright pink flowers on tall stems attract bees and butterflies.

Life cycle of a plant

- A seed falls on the ground.
- If the soil is good and the seed is watered, it begins to sprout.
- Roots push down into the soil.
- A green shoot pushes up above the soil.
- The shoot becomes the plant's stem.
- Leaves begin to grow. The leaves use water, sunlight and air to make food for the plant.
- The plant grows taller.
- Flowers buds grow. They open into flowers.

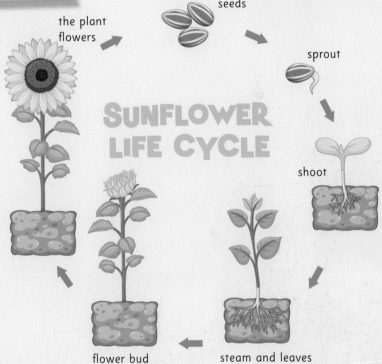

the plant flowers

seeds

sprout

shoot

SUNFLOWER LIFE CYCLE

flower bud

steam and leaves

- As the flowers die, seeds appear.
- The seeds blow in the wind or are carried by animals.
- They fall to the ground.
- A new plant begins to grow.

Grasslands

Grasslands are wide-open spaces in the countryside, covered in grass. In summer, bright red poppies and other flowers pop up all over grasslands. Some grasslands are under threat now. Farmers are using more **herbicides**, which can kill wild plants.

BEE ORCHID

Mimicry is when something pretends to be something else. The bee orchid gets its name because it looks like a bee! Its bee-shaped flower attracts bees to the plant so that **pollination** can take place (see page 15).

DAISY

Daisies come in all shapes and sizes. The common daisy, or lawn daisy, is a tiny white flower with a yellow middle. But many people think of it as a **weed**. This is because it spreads quickly on lawns and is hard to remove.

FOXGLOVES

Foxgloves have tube-shaped flowers that grow in a tall spike. Bees crawl right into the flowers to collect **nectar**.

COWSLIPS

Cowslips flower in the early spring. The flowers are like tubes. They are clustered together at the end of the stems. The leaves are wrinkled and tongue-shaped. Cowslips are becoming rarer as their habitats are being used for farming.

DANDELIONS

Dandelions have bright yellow flowers. The flowers open in the morning and close at night. Their seeds make a dandelion clock. The wind carries the seeds. They can travel for up to 8 kilometres!

COW PARSLEY

Cow parsley grows very quickly in the summer. It can reach up to a metre tall. It dies back in the winter. The tiny white flowers grow in clusters like umbrellas.

COCKSFOOT GRASS

This is a common type of grass. The long stalks and tufted flowerheads are a wonderful habitat for lots of minibeasts. Many caterpillars love to eat this grass!

CLOVER

Red clover grows close to the ground among grasses. Its flowerheads are pink balls of tiny tube-shaped flowers.

BUTTERCUPS

Buttercups have yellow cup-shaped flowers with five shiny petals. Buttercups look pretty but they have a strong, bitter taste. They are **poisonous** to some animals.

POPPIES

Bright red poppies pop up in the summer in grasslands and fields. The petals are silky and **delicate**. Poppy seeds can be used in cooking and baking.

How are seeds made?

petal

stamen { anther
         filament }

stigma

style

ovary

pistil

sepal

receptacle

peduncle

- Most plants start life as seeds. Flowerheads contain all the parts needed to make new seeds.

- Most flowers have both male and female parts. The male parts make pollen. The female parts make ovules, or eggs. The pollen and ovules need to come together to make seeds.

- The stamen is the male part of the flower. It is made of the filament and the anther.

- The pistil is the female part. It is made up of the stigma, style and ovary.

- Most flowers need help to move their pollen to their ovules.

- Nectar is a sweet liquid inside many flowers.

- Bees and butterflies feed on **nectar**. As they feed, pollen sticks to their bodies. They carry the pollen from the flowers' male parts to its female parts. Then seeds begin to form. The insects don't know it but they are helping to make new flowers! This is called **pollination**.

Bees feed on nectar.

15

Freshwater habitats

Freshwater habitats include rivers, streams, ponds, lakes and bogs. Some plants like the **moist** ground around rivers and ponds. Other plants actually grow in the water rather than in soil.

WATER CROWFOOT

Water crowfoot has some floating leaves. Others grow and stay under the water.

COTTON GRASS

Bogs are areas of wet, muddy ground. Cotton grass grows in pools of boggy water. Its roots have special air channels. The channels allow air to travel to the bottom of the roots. This stops the cotton grass from drowning.

DUCKWEED

Duckweed is a common sight on ponds and lakes. Its tiny round leaves float on the surface of the water. Little roots are attached to the leaves. The leaves can spread over a whole pond very quickly.

HART'S TONGUE FERN

This fern has long, tongue-shaped leaves with pointed tips. It grows in shady places near rivers and streams.

HAIRY WOOD-RUSH

Rushes grow in or near water. They have tall, hollow stems. Water travels up the stems. The hairy wood rush gets its name because it has three white, hairy stigmas.

HIMALAYAN BALSAM

This plant grows very tall and very quickly along river banks. Its flowers are shaped like helmets. The seed pods explode when they are ripe. Himalayan Balsam can smother other plants around it. This can cause those plants to die out. Many people are trying to get rid of it.

BULRUSHES

Bulrushes grow beside lakes and ponds. They are very tall with thick tough leaves. Their brown flowers are long and feel like velvet.

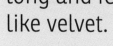

Along the coast

The coasts of the UK have beaches, sand dunes, rocky cliffs and salt marshes. Many small, tough plants grow in these places. Some plants even grow in the sea.

SEA HOLLY

Sea holly has prickly, silver-green leaves and a blue flower that looks like a thistle. Its roots grow deep into the sand. This helps it to stay upright in the wind.

MARSH SAMPHIRE

Salt marshes are areas of wet, salty ground near the sea. Many plants, such as marsh samphire, **thrive** here. It has thick, fleshy stems. Its tiny yellow flowers look like grains of sand.

MARRAM GRASS

Marram grass grows on sand dunes. It has spiky leaves and grows in clumps. Its roots help to hold the sand in place and stop it blowing away.

THRIFT

Also known as sea pink, thrift manages to survive on rocky cliffs. It has dark green leaves and round pink flowers.

SEASIDE DAISY

Seaside daisies have pink and purple flowers with yellow centres. They have hairy leaves. They grow in dry, rocky ground near the coast.

Where do plants come from?

Some plants are native to Britain. This means that they have grown naturally here since the last Ice Age, around 12,000 years ago. Other plants are non-native. They have been brought here from other countries. People bring them here to grow in gardens because they look nice. Seaside daisies were brought here from Central America. Now they grow wild in many places in the UK.

Some non-native plants can cause problems. Himalayan balsam (see page 17) has spread over many areas in the UK. It grows very quickly and crowds out other plants. It is now against the law to plant Himalayan balsam in the wild.

SILVERWEED

Silverweed grows on sand dunes. It has soft, silvery leaves. The leaves grow close to the ground. They stay green all year round. The yellow flowers appear in the summer.

SEA LETTUCE

This seaweed grows on rocks and in rockpools. It has large fleshy leaves. The leaves look floppy but are quite tough.

BLADDERWRACK

Bladderwrack is a type of seaweed. It grows in the sea. It has air bubbles along its fronds. These help it to float near the surface where sunlight is strongest. You might find it washed up on the beach.

What is seaweed?

There are many types of seaweed. They are not really plants. They are **algae**. Algae are like a simple type of plant.

Seaweed does not have roots. Some have holdfasts, which look like roots. These help to keep the seaweed in one place. But the holdfasts do not take in **nutrients** like plant roots do. Seaweed takes in water and nutrients through the whole of its structure.

Algae need sunlight to make food, just like plants. So they often grow in shallow water where the sunlight reaches below the surface.

LICHEN

Lichen is made up of a **fungus** and an alga living together. The alga produces food and the fungus gathers water. Lichen can grow over rocks on sunny clifftops.

Heathland and mountains

Heathland is wild open countryside. It is often covered in **shrubs** and heather. Heathlands are important wildlife habitats. Snakes, lizards and minibeasts make their home there. Birds build their nests on the ground. Mountains are also wild habitats. It often gets cold at the top of mountains. Plants that grow here need to be tough to survive the bad weather.

MOSS CAMPION

Moss campion grows in a cushion shape. The "cushion" absorbs heat from the sun. This keeps it warm in cold temperatures.

HEATHER

Purple heather is a tough plant. It can survive windy weather and poor soil. Deer and sheep **graze** on heather.

GORSE

Gorse is a spiny shrub. Its leaves are like sharp needles. It has yellow flowers. It grows in wild heathlands. Gorse provides shelter for many insects and birds.

ROUND-LEAVED SUNDEW

This is a **carnivorous** plant. It eats insects! Each leaf has red hairs that are covered in liquid. The liquid is very sticky. If an insect lands on a leaf, the hairs curl round to trap the insect. Then the whole leaf curls round the insect. The plant then **digests** the insect.

BRACKEN

Bracken is a type of fern. Ferns are flowerless green plants. They have feather-like leaves called fronds. Bracken grows on heathland and on hillsides. Its green fronds are tightly curled when they first appear. Then they unfurl. In autumn, bracken turns brown and orange, and dies back.

SAXIFRAGE

This plant grows well on rock faces high in the hills. Purple saxifrage has purple flowers with five petals. Some types of saxifrage grow only on the highest mountains in Scotland.

Towns and cities

Flowers and plants don't only grow wild in the countryside. Many plants **thrive** in the city. Some are planted in parks and gardens. But many also find homes on walls, in cracks in pavements, on railway tracks and in disused buildings. Some people call them **weeds** but they provide habitats and food for minibeasts and birds.

STINGING NETTLES

Stinging nettles grow all over the place. They can be seen growing on unused land. Nettles have hairs that are like needles. They give out a liquid when they are touched. The liquid can cause a bumpy, itchy rash.

BUDDLEIA

Buddleia can often be spotted growing in sunny spots beside railways. It can grow in poor soil. It is also known as the "butterfly bush". This is because its white or purple flowers attract butterflies. They lay their eggs on the leaves. The caterpillars eat the leaves when they hatch.

PEARLWORT

The flowers on pearlwort don't have any petals. This green plant grows in the cracks in paths and along the tops of walls.

HAIRY BITTERCRESS

This dark green plant with tiny white flowers spreads across walls or on pavements. Seeds explode from the plant and can spread a long distance.

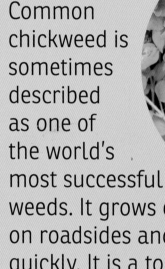

CHICKWEED

Common chickweed is sometimes described as one of the world's most successful weeds. It grows easily on roadsides and spreads quickly. It is a tough plant and can even produce flowers under snow!

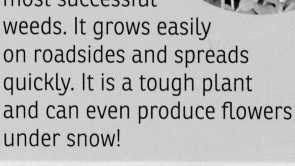

IVY-LEAVED TOADFLAX

This is a climbing plant that creeps over walls and pavements. Its roots grow into the little cracks and holes between bricks and paving slabs. It has pretty little purple flowers. Its stalks have a red colour.

Parks and gardens

The plants in parks and gardens are not usually wild. They are planted by gardeners. Often, these are plants from other countries that would not survive well in the wild in the UK. But they grow well if someone cares for them.

DAFFODILS, TULIPS AND CROCUSES

Plants grown from **bulbs** are often one of the first signs of spring. Daffodils, tulips and crocuses look bright and colourful. They die back after spring but they will come back the next year if the bulbs are left in the soil.

LILIES

Lilies have large, beautiful flowers and a strong smell. They grow well in pots.

LAVENDER

Lavender is often grown in gardens. Its purple flowers and strong **scent** attract bees. The flowers can be dried and kept inside to make your house smell nice.

What are bulbs?

Some plants grow from bulbs, not seeds. Bulbs come in different shapes and sizes. Food for the plant is stored inside them. In the spring, green shoots sprout from them. Daffodils, tulips, crocuses and lilies grow from bulbs.

daffodil bulbs

HERBS

Herbs are small, leafy plants that we eat. They come in many different flavours. Basil makes a delicious pizza topping. Mint is tasty in ice cream! Herbs are easy to grow – you can even grow them inside on a windowsill.

GARDEN SHRUBS

Shrubs are plants that have woody stems, but they are smaller than trees. Hydrangeas and lilacs are common garden shrubs. Their pretty flowers can be purple, blue, pink and white.

hydrangea

What are weeds?

Weeds are unwanted plants, such as nettles, dandelions and chickweed. They grow and spread quickly. They can take the space, water, light and **nutrients** that other plants need. Gardeners spend a lot of time digging up weeds. This helps protect the plants they want to grow.

ROSES

Roses are bushes covered in large, beautiful flowers. The flowers can be red, white, yellow, pink or purple. Prickles cover the stems. Rose petals have a pretty **scent** (smell). They are used to add flavour to water, perfume and sweets.

CLIMBERS

Climbers are plants that "climb" up walls and fences as they grow. Sweet peas have pink or purple flowers. They grow to around 2 metres tall, which is taller than most people! Honeysuckle and passion flowers are also climbers.

sweet pea

passion flower

EDIBLE FLOWERS

We all eat fruit and vegetables, which we get from plants. The petals of some flowers are also edible. Courgette flowers can be eaten.

courgette

FRUIT AND VEGETABLES

Many people like to grow fruit and vegetables to eat. Cauliflowers, carrots, cabbages and potatoes need to be watered well. They also need to be protected from birds, caterpillars and slugs. Strawberries and rhubarb can be grown and then made into jams and puddings.

strawberry

What are houseplants?

Some plants cannot live outside in this country. People grow houseplants, such as cacti, succulents and ferns, in pots in their homes.

Glossary

alga simple plant that has no flowers, usually found in water

bulb underground food storage for a plant; some plants grow from bulbs

carnivorous eats meat

delicate easily damaged

digest to break down food so it can be used as energy

fungus organism that produces spores; fungi are not plants; mushrooms and toadstools are types of fungus

graze to eat grass

herbicide chemical used to kill weeds

moist damp

nectar sugary liquid found in flowers

nutrient substance that is important for life and growth

photosynthesis way that green plants use sunlight to make food and carbon dioxide

poisonous harmful if eaten

pollination movement of pollen from the male part of the flower to the female part; after pollination, seeds can begin to form

scent smell

shrub plant with a woody stem, smaller than a tree

thrive live and grow well

weed unwanted plant

Find out more

Books

Roots, Stems, Leaves and Flowers: All About Plant Parts, Ruth Owen (Ruby Tuesday Books, 2016)

RSPB First Book of Flowers, Anita Ganeri and David Chandler (A & C Black Children's Books, 2011)

Websites

www.bbc.co.uk/education/clips/z3wsbk7
Watch a video on the life cycle of a plant at this BBC website.

www.woodlandtrust.org.uk/visiting-woods/trees-woods-and-wildlife/ plants-and-fungi/woodland-wildflowers/
Visit the Woodland Trust's website to discover many more types of woodland flowers.

Index

algae 21

bladderwrack 20
bluebells 6
bracken 23
brambles 9
buddleia 24
bulbs 27
bulrushes 17
buttercups 14

chickweed 25, 28
climbers 28
clover 14
cocksfoot grass 14
cotton grass 16
cow parsley 13
cowslips 13

daffodils, tulips and crocuses 26
daisies 12, 19
dandelions 13, 28
deadly nightshade 8
duckweed 16

edible flowers 29

fly agaric 8
forget-me-nots 7
foxgloves 13
fruit and vegetables 29

garden shrubs 27
goosegrass 10
gorse 23

habitats 4–5
hairy bittercress 25
hairy wood-rush 17
hart's tongue fern 17
heather 22
herbs 27
Himalayan balsam 17, 19
houseplants 29

ivy 10
ivy-leaved toadflax 25

lavender 26

lichen 21
life cycle of a plant 11
lilies 26
lilies of the valley 7
lords and ladies 7

marram grass 18
marsh samphire 18
mistletoe 8
moss 9
moss campion 22

native plants 19

orchids 7, 12

pearlwort 25
poisonous plants 8
poppies 14
primroses 6

red campion 11
requirements for growth 5
roses 28
round-leaved sundew 23

saxifrage 23
sea holly 18
sea lettuce 20
seaweed 20, 21
seeds 15
silverweed 20
snake's head fritillaries 7
snowdrops 10
stinging nettles 24, 28

thrift 19
toadstools 8

water crowfoot 16

weeds 28
wild garlic 6
wood anemones 7

yellow brain fungus 9